David Porteous Art and Craft Books

Silk Painting

Vibeke Born

DAVID PORTEOUS
CHUDLEIGH · DEVON

Contents

Introduction

Most people are amazed when they start painting on silk and discover the magical effects they can achieve. It is wonderful seeing the way that the paints flow on the silk, almost like watching oil floating on water.

I am often asked if it's difficult to paint on silk, and the simple answer is 'no'. However, silk painting does require you to use a range of techniques, and it needs both patience and accuracy if you are to achieve pleasing results.

The first sections of this book describe the techniques you will use and the equipment and materials you will need, and if you have not done any silk painting before, it is important to read these carefully. Here you will learn about the different kinds of silk, the paints, how to prepare the silk by stretching it over a frame, the best brushes to use and so forth. We also suggest some techniques that you should bear in mind if you haven't used silk paints before. You will learn, among other things, how to achieve brilliant and unexpected results with a microwave oven. Even if you have used silk paints before, you are sure to find some useful tips in these pages.

All the pieces illustrated in this book were decorated with steam-fixed paints, which often give richer and denser colours than the iron-fixed paints. Many people think that steam-fixed paints are only suitable for 'professionals', but this is a notion that this book sets out to dispel. However, the projects can just as easily be done with the excellent range of iron-fixed paints now available.

Although the projects included here explain how to decorate scarves, many of the designs are intended to be displayed as wall-hangings or even cushion covers, and instructions on mounting the finished paintings are included here. It is almost a shame to use these patterns as scarves, because the exciting designs cannot be seen clearly when they are worn, but if you prefer painting scarves to working on pictures for hanging, you could, of course, simplify the patterns.

The motifs shown in the book can be drawn free-hand, but one of the most appealing aspects of silk painting is that you do not need to be a brilliant artist to achieve first-class results. It is the paints themselves and their effect on the silk that make the finished product so splendid. Nor does it matter if the motifs are slightly distorted – quite the opposite, for this can make your paintings even more exciting and artistic.

However, if you want to transfer the motifs directly, we explain how you can enlarge the paintings before transferring them to the silk. This could not be easier if you have access to a photocopying machine capable of making enlargements, and you can, of course, always use the grid method if you cannot get to a photocopier. There are also single-motif templates with each painting. These can be used in many ways and in a variety of combinations, not just the ways illustrated here, and they are also ideal for cards and small pictures, which are excellent projects for beginners to try out the processes and for more experienced silk painters to experiment with different colours or makes of paint.

For best results, read through the descriptions of the various materials from the beginning. The projects become more complicated as the book progresses, so that you can gradually increase your expertise as you go along.

I hope that the techniques shown in this book and the designs will inspire both new and experienced silk painters to try this exciting medium.
Have fun.

Vibeke Born

Silks

There are many different kinds of silk and all of them can be used for silk painting. Some of the many types you can use are described below.

If you are not sure whether a piece of material is silk, which is a completely natural fabric, you can test it by setting light to one of the corners. If the material melts and forms a hard edge, it is a synthetic fabric. If, on the other hand, the material smells like burnt hair when it is set alight, it is silk.

Silk is sold according to weight per square metre (yard), and you can, of course, buy some types of silk in the form of ready-made items – scarves, blouses and so on. It is not worth the effort of making a scarf yourself because it takes a long time to make the rolled edging, but you can save a great deal of money by making blouses and other items of clothing from lengths of silk you have decorated yourself instead of buying them ready-made.

Paj

This is the thinnest silk you can buy, and it is often used because it is cheap. It is sold by the metre and is frequently used for scarves. Paj silk is good for testing small patches of colour, but it cannot be recommended for larger jobs. It is translucent, crumples easily and the paint dries too quickly, leaving unwanted and unattractive blotches. It is therefore better to use a stronger silk such as habutai.

Habutai

This can be bought in a variety of weights – light, medium and heavyweight – and it is good to paint on because the colours become deep and dense. Habutai silk can be used for almost anything – scarves, pictures, clothes and so on. If you have not painted on silk before, you should choose habutai for the best possible results. Although it is slightly more expensive than paj silk, it repays the extra costs in terms of results. You can buy lengths of habutai from haberdashers, and it is often used for a variety of ready-made articles that you can decorate yourself.

Twill

This is a fine to medium weight, strong silk, with a distinctive diagonal weave, which is not to everyone's taste. It is stronger and more expensive than habutai, and it is normally sold only as scarves or ties.

Satin

This material has a beautiful shiny surface, and it is very useful for pictures, small ornaments and special articles of clothing. The colour of silk paint is beautifully deep because of the dense weave. Unlike the silks previously mentioned, this one has a right and a wrong side. The front is shiny. It is sold by the metre and as ready-made articles.

Crepe de Chine

This kind of silk, available in weights from light to heavy, has a plain weave and is not prone to crumpling. It is very flexible and is especially useful for clothes. Crepe de Chine absorbs a great deal of colour and 'gives' while you apply the paint, which means that you have to tighten it several times during the process. It is sold both by the metre and as ready-made articles.

Crepe Satin

This is a rich and fairly expensive silk that is suitable for clothes. The front and back are quite different. The front is shiny and the back is crepe. It is sold by the metre and as ready-made designs.

Georgette

This transparent, light fabric does not crumple easily. The silk falls nicely and is best suited for skirts, dresses and long scarves. It is sold by the metre and as scarves.

Tussah or Wild Silk

This is a strong fabric that is used for cushions, clothes, jackets, trousers and other items exposed to wear and tear. This silk is not suitable for stretching and using with gutta because the weave is not uniform.

Paints

Silk paints are lovely to work with. They are highly concentrated and each small pot will last you for a long time. Occasionally you may have to thin the paints before you use them, because they are very rich in pigments. If possible, do not use water straight from the tap, because it is too hard. Instead, use distilled water or water that has boiled and then allowed to cool. Use a cheap plastic pipette (see illustration) to draw up the paint and water. Clean the pipette in a weak solution of bleach and water.

There are two types of silk paint – iron-fixed paint (pigment paint) and steam-fixed paint (reactive paint).

Steam-fixed paints are sometimes regarded as the 'real' silk paints because they penetrate the fibre of the silk and give depth to the painting. Iron-fixed paints rest of the surface of the fibres and do not penetrate them. This gives the painting a reverse side and sometimes the colours do not altogether do justice either to themselves or to the silk.

When the silk has been painted, the paint has to be fixed so that the colours do not run when the silk is washed or gets damp. As we have noted, the paints can be iron-fixed or steam-fixed, and it is important to decide before you begin which method of fixing you will use because that determines which paints you should use. Small cards and pictures painted with steam-fixed colours do not need to be fixed because they are not exposed to moisture, but they may tend to fade faster if unfixed.

Iron-fixed Paints

These paints are fixed by ironing the silk on the back with a warm iron or by placing it in an oven at about 130°C (270°F) (see page 18). This method of fixing is slightly easier than steam-fixing (see overleaf and page 18), but the main disadvantage to using iron-fixed paints compared with steam-fixed paints is that the paint tends to smudge, especially on larger surfaces. However, the main advantage of iron-fixed paints is that they can be used on all types of material, unlike steam-fixed paints, which can be used only on silk and some types of wool.

Steam-fixed Paints

These paints are fixed using steam (see page 18). This method of fixing is slightly more difficult than simply ironing the paints. On the other hand they are easy to work with because they flow more smoothly than iron-fixed paints. This means that it is easier to create an even surface.

The two types of paint cannot be blended together on the silk when they are wet. However, if you have any iron-fixed paint left over, it can be painted onto a dry steam-fixed paint, used as a base colour. Iron-fixed paint can also be used on white border sections of the same piece of silk as steam-fixed paints.

Before steam-fixing the silk it is very important to iron the back to fix the pigments in the paint.

All the designs in this book have been created using steam-fixed paints. There are many different brands available for silk painting, and you may find that you are happier working with one kind of paint than another, so it is worth experimenting with different kinds to find out which you prefer.

Gutta

Because silk paints would simply run all over the surface of the fabric and into each other, they need to be contained within barriers. Gutta is used as an edge marker to stop the paints running together on the silk, and in this way the paint can be concentrated in defined areas, which is one of the reasons that silk paints give such vibrant colours. The use of gutta also makes it possible to paint a motif accurately in defined colour sections, almost as if within the outlines drawn on a piece of paper.

Two types of gutta are available – water-based and spirit-based – and there are advantages and disadvantages to each kind, so it is best to try both and find which you prefer.

Water-based Gutta

There is a water-based gutta for iron-fixing and another for steam-fixing, although gutta for steam-fixing can be used for iron-fixing. Some of the advantages of water-based gutta are:
• It does not smell
• It can be washed out once the silk is fixed.
• It can easily be thinned with water. (Do not thin too much.)

The disadvantages are:
• It may takes several hours to dry, depending on the thickness of the line drawn.
• It can be difficult to draw a thin, fine line because some brands of gutta have a tendency to run slightly.
• If you apply paint to the surface on one side of a gutta line before the paint on the other side of the line is perfectly dry, the gutta may dissolve. The same applies when you paint several coats on the same spot. It is therefore advisable to let each application of paint dry thoroughly before applying the next colour.

Spirit-based Gutta

This kind of gutta can be used for both fixing methods. The advantages of spirit-based gutta are:

- It dries very quickly.
- It is fairly easy to produce fine, smooth lines.
- It never dissolves in paint, even when the paints are applied before the first colour is dry.

The disadvantages of spirit-based gutta are:

- It smells a little.
- It has to be removed by leaving the silk to soak in a dry-cleaning fluid for about 20 minutes, then hanging it out to dry in fresh air. If you are not keen on this method, you can send the silk to be professionally dry cleaned. If the gutta is not thoroughly removed, there is a danger that it could become rubbery.
- It has to be thinned with a special diluent. Check the manufacturer's instructions for the diluent that should be used with the particular brand of paint that you are using.

All the articles illustrated in this book were decorated with spirit-based gutta.

Coloured Gutta

In addition to the basic clear version, water-based gutta is available in a range of colours and in gold, silver and black. They can be tricky to work with as they sometimes crack or small pieces chip off. Coloured gutta has not been used in this book – for those very reasons! If you do use them follow the manufactuter's instructions carefully.

Spirit-based gutta for steam-fixing is available in black, gold and silver. These can also be tricky to work with, and coloured gutta is recommended only for heavy silks on which it should be able to penetrate right into the silk without leaving behind a rubbery deposit.

It is important that the gutta is the right consistency when it is applied. If it is too thin, it will not create an effective barrier; if it is too thick, it will stay on top of the silk without penetrating into the fibres. Coloured gutta for steam-fixing should not be left soaking in the cleaning fluid nor sent to the cleaner's as the coloured line will disappear.

Gold and silver quickly lose their sheen if the silk is washed frequently. It is therefore best to use gold and silver gutta for cards or pictures or for small effects on scarves.

Stretching Silk Over a Frame

Before you can start painting on the silk, you have to stretch it over a frame so that the surface is taut and free from creases and so that it is raised above your working surface.

There are some occasions when the silk does not need to be stretched; see pages 24–7.

Frames

Some craft shops stock special frames for stretching silk. These are of various types and sizes, and it is even possible to obtain frames that can be adjusted to accommodate a range of sizes.

It is important that the silk is raised clear of the table and is free of the base. If it is not, the gutta will not flow smoothly over the surface of the fabric. The heights of ready-made frames are generally adjusted by four wing nuts, and you can also buy small blocks to raise the frame further. One of the easiest ways of increasing the height of the frame so that it is comfortable for you to work at is to cut four equal lengths

from a piece of wooden dowel and to fix them to the frame as illustrated below.

If you are a beginner and do not want to buy a purpose-made frame to start with, you could use an old picture frame or, if the piece you are decorating is small, an embroidery frame.

When you are working on larger pieces of material, such as a long scarf, you could make a frame by using table trestles or the trestles used for decorating and two strips of wood. It is important that the trestle tops are made of wood so that the strips can be nailed securely to them (see the illustration).

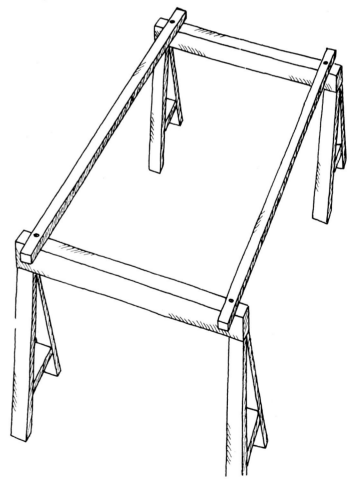

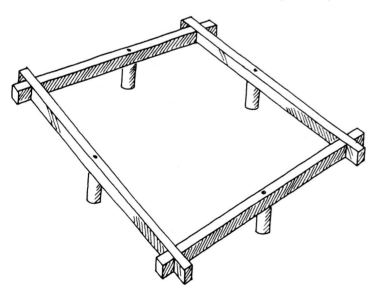

Stretching

Before stretching the silk over the frame, cover the top edges of the frame with masking tape or something similar to stop the silk paint seeping down into the wood. If you do not do this, the paint might come off when you are using the frame for something different and spoil it. The tape can be changed as often as necessary.

It is extremely important to make sure that the silk is taut and smooth before you begin work. The fabric is held in place with special three-pronged pins. Do not use drawing pins, which will leave holes in the fabric.

Starting in one corner, begin to insert pins along one of the long sides, leaving 15–20cm (6–8in) between each pin all the way round. Then insert more pins so that there is only about 5cm (2in) between each one. Aim to arrange the pins so that they are not exactly opposite each other, which helps to prevent ridges forming in the fabric.

If you are decorating a ready-made scarf that has already got a rolled edge, position each pin so that only one of the prongs is actually in the silk while the other two are in the wooden frame (as shown in the illustration). This helps to avoid making holes in the silk. If you are working on silk that is going to be made up into, say, a cushion cover, insert all three prongs into to fabric as shown below.

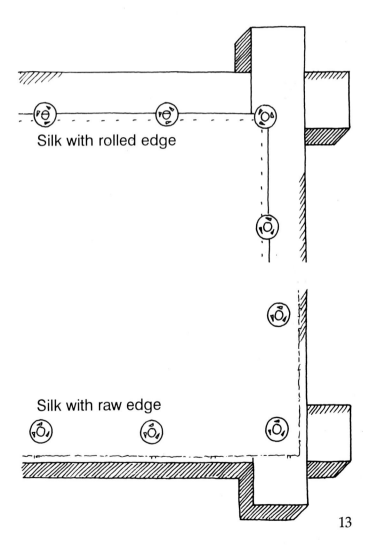

Silk with rolled edge

Silk with raw edge

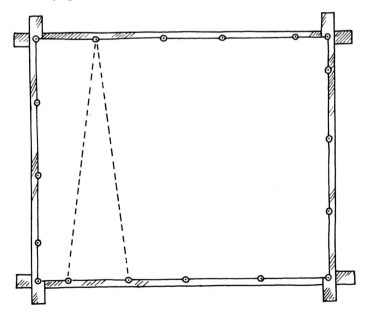

13

Applying Gutta

Gutta can be applied from a special bottle with a nozzle into which metal nibs can be inserted for especially fine or detailed work. The nibs are available in several sizes, and you may need to hold the nib in place in the nozzle with a small piece of masking tape.

Unscrew the cap and fill the bottle with gutta. It is easiest to apply gutta when the bottle is about three-quarters full. You should try to prevent air from coming out with the gutta, because this causes gaps in the lines you draw, through which the paint will seep. Hold the bottle as you would a pen, with the nozzle just resting on the surface of the silk.

The consistency of the gutta will depend on the type of silk you are using. You will have to experiment for yourself, but in general, the finer the silk, the thicker the gutta should be. Before you apply the gutta to the silk, it is a good idea to test a small piece of scrap silk to see whether the consistency is right.

When you use gutta to draw a motif on silk, the silk must always be supported and stretched in a frame. The fabric must not be allowed to rest on your working surface or the gutta will not flow smoothly over the material. The fabric must also be absolutely dry before you begin to apply the gutta to the silk.

Do not work too slowly or the gutta line will be too thick. On the other hand, if you work too quickly, the line may break so that the paint is not held within the shapes you have drawn. Try to apply the gutta with a smooth, fairly fast action. You will find that, with practice, you soon learn how to apply a smooth, even line.

Where lines of gutta meet it is important to make sure that they overlap (see the illustration).

If you make a mistake, remove the gutta with a cottonwool bud dipped in water, white spirit or the manufacturer's recommended diluent.

Only apply the paint when the gutta is completely

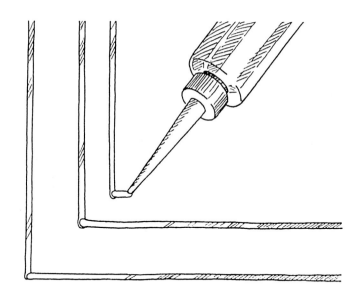

dry. Use a hair-drier if you want to begin work straight way. Otherwise leave the gutta for about 24 hours.

When you are painting on silk with gutta, do not apply paint right up to the gutta line because the paint will flow outwards of its own accord. If you go too close to the line, the paint could easily flow over and into another section.

Storing Gutta

Water-based gutta can be stored easily. If it becomes too thick, simply thin it will a little water.

Storing spirit-based gutta is more difficult because the spirit evaporates very quickly. You cannot simply leave the gutta in the nozzle-topped bottle. There are three possible solutions. Replace the nozzle with a screw cap. Pour unused gutta back into its original container. Keep the nozzle-topped container in a large screw-top jar.

If you have used a metal nib, replace the wire when you have finished work so that the nib does not get clogged up with dried gutta.

Brushes

To achieve a good result, you must use the right brushes. As with all tools, it is usually far more economical to buy one or two of the best brushes you can afford and to look after them properly than to buy several cheap ones. At first, however, you may want to experiment with synthetic brushes, which cost about half as much as the best bristle brushes.

Brushes are graded numerically, the lower numbers indicating the finer points. Craft and art supply shops will stock a wide range of sizes and qualities. Choose a brush that will hold a large amount of paint so that you don't have to keep dipping it all the time. It is also important to ensure that the brush has a well-defined point and does not become untidy when you paint with it.

For most silk paints you will need a good quality no. 12 watercolour brush. When you really get bitten by the silk painting bug, you will find that it is easier to have several brushes so that you do not have to wash your brush before you use a new colour.

For larger jobs you could use a no. 18 silk painting brush, but if you are painting large areas with a single colour you can buy foam rubber 'brushes', which consist of shaped pieces of foam rubber on a handle. These 'brushes' are very cheap and are available in several widths.

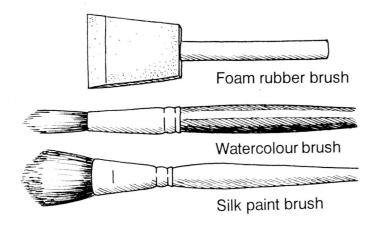

Foam rubber brush

Watercolour brush

Silk paint brush

Applying the Paint

Before you begin, pour the paint you want to use into a small bowl or jar. You can also buy special palettes that have sections to keep different colours separate. Never dip your brush straight into the pot in which you bought the paint, because the slightest residue of another paint on the brush will contaminate the paint in the jar.

Before you begin to paint, make sure that you have sufficient paint – it is better to have too much than too little because it is almost impossible to re-create a shade that you have made by blending or thinning.

Large, Even Surfaces

If you are painting a large area, you need to dip your brush into the paint frequently. Start by working outwards from one corner with soft, even strokes. The strokes should not be too long and they should always be in the same direction and never crisscross. It is easiest to achieve an even surface if the paint is not too thin, but this will partly depend on the type of silk. On a fairly fine silk, for example, the paint dries almost while you are applying it.

Let one colour dry before you apply a new colour unless otherwise stated in the text. The same rule applies when you apply gutta to a painted surface. Gutta will adhere only to a dry surface.

To make sure that a surface is quite dry, test it with the back of your hand, which is much more sensitive than your fingertips. If the silk feels cold, it is still damp.

It is also possible to colour large pieces of silk in the washing machine with the new washing machine paints for natural fabrics. This method is ideal, for example, for the materials for dresses, blouses and other things that cannot be stretched over a frame. Follow the manufacturer's instructions.

Transferring Motifs

When you draw a motif on a piece of silk, use a water-erasable fabric pen or a special fabric marker. The 'ink' in these markers, which resemble felt-tipped pens, disappears after a day or two.

You can easily transfer a design or motif by placing the original on the table, holding it in place with small pieces of tape in the corners, and then using low-tack masking tape or fabric tape to hold the silk in position over it. Provided it has been clearly drawn, the line of the motif will be visible through the silk. Now draw the whole motif with the fabric marker. Don't leave it too long before you paint the motif or the line may disappear.

If you want to paint an all-over background colour on the silk to stop the lines of gutta showing white, paint the background first and then draw the motif when the silk is already in the frame. The motif can be held, by tape, behind the silk.

If you want to enlarge the motifs that have been used for the projects illustrated in this book, you can do so with a photocopying machine. All the motifs have been drawn to the same scale and have been designed to be

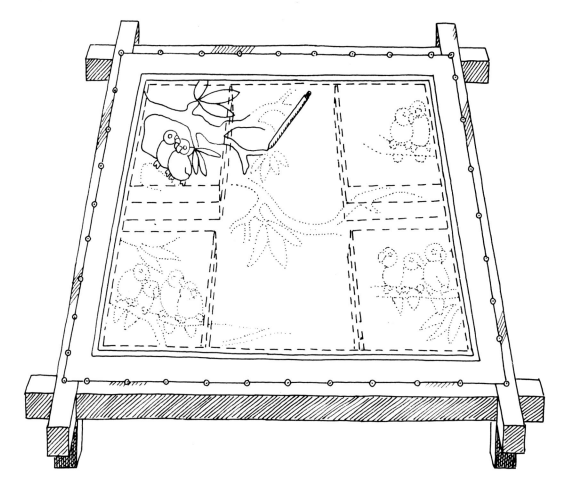

the correct size for a 90 x 90cm (36 x 36in) scarf excluding gutta frames.

- Place a piece of tracing paper over the motif and draw it without gutta frames
- Divide the motif into 16 equal squares
- Enlarge each square by 141 per cent on a photocopying machine – four times in all
- Tape the 16 large copies together.

If you turn the square through 90 degrees each time you make a copy, you will stop the motif becoming distorted in the photocopying machine.

If you cannot get to a photocopying machine, use the grid method. Trace the motif then draw over it a grid of equally spaced vertical and horizontal squares. On a clean sheet of paper, draw a grid that has squares that are four times as large as the original grid and transfer the motif, square by corresponding square.

Fixing

When you have applied the paints to the silk, you should fix them so that the paint does not run when you wash the silk or if it gets damp some other way. As we have noted, silk paints can be either iron-fixed or steam-fixed. It depends on the paint used.

After painting the silk, you should wait for at least 24 hours to allow the paints to set. Painted silk that has not been fixed should always be kept in a plastic bag so that it does not inadvertently get wet or damp. Even the smallest drop of water can ruin your work.

Iron-fixing

If you are using gutta, it is easiest to put the silk in an oven, pre-heated to 130°C (270°F). Roll the silk in clean, absorbent paper, making sure that the gutta lines do not come in contact with each other. Fold the roll in the middle as shown in the illustration and place it in the oven on a baking tray for about 10 minutes. Switch off the oven the moment you put the silk in. If you want to fix the silk with an iron, place some baking parchment or greaseproof paper over the back of the silk. Then iron over the paper for about 3 minutes. The iron should be set for wool or cotton.

Steam-fixing

Manufacturers and suppliers of silk paints can usually advise about places where you can get your work fixed professionally, and if you have worked on a large or especially intricate piece, it is advisable to seek professional help.

If you have a pressure cooker it is possible to replicate in a small way the system employed by professional steamers, although this method is suitable only for small pieces. Place each piece on several pieces of absorbent paper and make sure there are no creases in the fabric. Cover the silk with several more pieces. Tape the ends of the paper together and then roll up the paper to make a small, squarish package. Place the package in a basket suspended above 5–7.5cm (2–3in) of boiling water. It is important that the package doesn't touch the sides of the pressure cooker because the condensation would mark the silk. Cover the basket with more paper and wrap a piece of aluminium foil over it. Boil under pressure for about 45 minutes.

There is another method of steam-fixing paints, and this involves the use of chemicals. The silk is placed in a cold solution of special chemicals. This method is not suitable if you have used a lot of paint because there is a danger that the paints might run and that pale areas become discoloured. The chemicals required to make the fixing solution are available in hobby shops, but they are quite expensive, and the method is really suitable only for small articles like hair scrunchies.

Small cards and pictures painted with steam-fixed paints do not need to be fixed because they are not exposed to moisture, although the process of fixing makes the silk more brilliant and the colours more intense and light-fast.

The silk should be washed after fixing to remove water-based gutta. Spirit-based gutta can be removed with the special cleaning fluid available from paint manufacturers, or it can taken to be dry cleaned.

Washing and Ironing

If you use steam-fix paints without thinning them, you will find there is a certain amount of excess that needs to be washed out. Washing also makes the silk bright and soft.

Before you begin, have some old, clean towels ready to roll the washed silk in. You may find that some colour comes off on the towels.

First, wash the silk in cold water with a little vinegar added. Then put the silk into some water with some washing powder – the kind recommended for wool is best. Do not leave it to soak, but wash the fabric quickly, before rinsing again in the solution of vinegar. Then roll it in the towels. If a lot of colour came out in the vinegar water after the first wash, change it before the final rinse. If the water-based gutta does not completely disappear in the first wash, it will go in the next wash.

You must roll the silk in the towels, which will absorb the moisture. It's important that the painted surfaces of the silk are not left to dry while they are folded against each other or the paint will simply smudge and the colours will merge. Finally, iron the silk until it is completely dry. Do not hang the wet silk up to dry, because paint will run down the silk.

Instead of washing the silk by hand, you can take it to be dry cleaned. Ties should always be dry cleaned.

Unroll the towels and iron the silk dry from the back. The iron should be set for wool. Scarves, which will be used later for pictures, can be rolled on poster tubes to avoid folds.

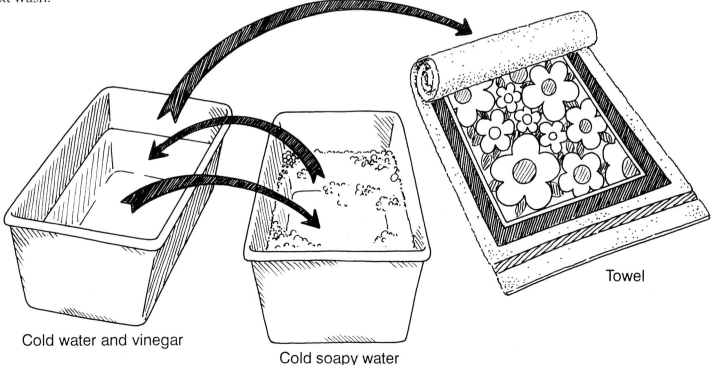

Cold water and vinegar

Cold soapy water

Towel

Getting Started

Your first attempts at painting on silk will require only a few pieces of equipment. If you are really bitten by the silk painting bug, you can acquire more paints and materials later.

In addition to a piece of habutai silk (see page 8) and a no. 12 watercolour brush (see page 15) you will, of course, need silk paints.

Paints

Silk paints come in a wide range of colours, a selection of which are shown on this page.

At first, however, you need only acquire seven colours: yellow, mandarin orange, pink, azure blue, dark blue, emerald green and black. By mixing the paints you can create many different colours, some of which are shown opposite.

Start with the pale paint and mix the dark colour in until you achieve the shade you want. Use the pipette to draw up the paints and mix them in separate small dishes or a special palette.

On page 22 are three examples of the ways in which paints react when they come in contact with silk.

Sienna

Brown

Grey

Black

Yellow

Mandarin orange

Orange

Red

Cyclamen

Pink

Mauve

Dark blue

Blue

Azure blue

Turquoise

Emerald green

Moss green

Dark green

Green-yellow

Ochre

Thin the paints with cold, boiled or distilled water. Plastic pipettes are cheap and absolutely essential for sucking up blended or thinned paints.

When you are painting and mixing colours, use the pure yellow with care. Although yellow is excellent for using with other colours to create new shades, it can be a very cold colour and should sometimes be used in moderation compared with, say, the mandarin orange, which is much warmer.

If you need a grey paint, it is not enough just to thin the black. You should buy a ready-mixed grey. If you are going to use black, it is a good idea to pour some paint into a small bowl or jar a few hours before you intend to use it. That way some of the water will evaporate and the black will be extra concentrated.

If you are painting a large area, mix plenty of paint. It is almost impossible to re-create a particular tone, achieved either by thinning or mixing, and there is nothing more frustrating than to find that you run out before you have finished properly.

You can keep left-over paint in small screw-top jars of the kind that are used for mustard and so on.

The Properties of Paint

These three examples illustrate the ways in which the paints react when they come in contact with the silk. Depending on how you apply the paint, you can achieve a range of effects. When you use gutta to create sections, the colours are highly concentrated, as you can see in sample 1 below. If you apply the paints wet on wet as in sample 2, they flow into one another and blend, merging into each other and forming sub-

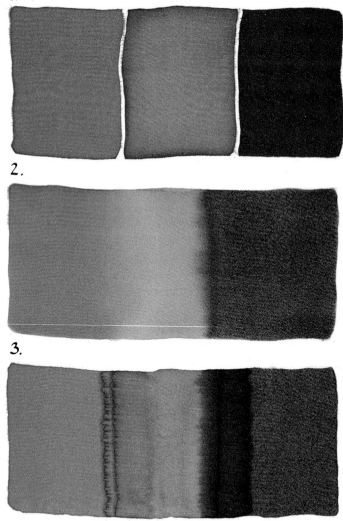

1.

2.

3.

tle tones. If you let the paints dry between each coat, the borders are sharper and more clearly defined, as in sample 3.

Mounting

Small silk paintings or pieces that you have used as experiments can be mounted and inserted in frames.

Many craft and art supply shops sell blank cards. These usually take the form of a piece of card with two folds. The silk is placed on the centre panel and the front panel, which has an aperture cut in it, is folded over and held in place with glue or double-sided tape. The silk should be trimmed so that there is sufficient margin to hold it in place around the edge. Use a fabric adhesive sparingly, and keep the adhesive as far away from the visible section of the silk as possible. You may want to add a small amount of lightweight wadding behind the silk.

Silk paintings can also be mounted in picture frames. Make sure that the edge of the painting is not a vital part of the composition because it will be hidden behind the mount. Again, use fabric adhesive or low-tack spray adhesive to hold the painting on the backing card and experiment before you glue to make sure that the area visible within the mount is the section you want to be on view. Assemble the frame according to the manufacturer's instructions.

If the edge of the silk is an integral part of the design, you might want to consider using two pieces of glass or perspex (or plexiglass, which is lighter). The entire piece of silk is held between the two pieces of glass, which are held together with various styles of corner and side fixtures, which will probably include a hanger so that you can display the painting on a wall.

Wherever you display your work, make sure that it is not in direct sunlight, which will cause the colours to fade.

Silk Painting for Children

Silk painting is a wonderful occupation for children, as it is for elderly people.

Children are quick and impulsive, and there seems to be no limit to the amount of silk and paints that they can use up in a fairly short space of time unless they are given specific tasks to work on. Most children greatly enjoy drawing and painting, and can produce some really amazing work.

Always supervise children carefully because some paints and gutta are slightly toxic. Follow the manufacturer's instructions.

Many elderly people, on the other hand, are 'frightened' of painting on silk. However, once they get used to working with the paint and with gutta they can produce some really beautiful things.

If elderly people find it difficult to hold paintbrushes, the colour can be laid on the silk by means of a plastic pipette. Laying the silk across a piece of wadding can also make it easier to work with the paints.

Working with Children

Although it is tempting, never expect children to work with cheap materials. It is far better to let them use lots of small pieces of good quality silk than to give them large pieces of poorer quality fabric. It is a great fallacy to assume that children should work with cheaper materials than adults. With silk particularly, the results that can be achieved on fine silks are so very different from those that can be achieved on coarse fabric that it can be dispiriting for children if the results are not as good as they have seen elsewhere. Often children who work with good materials are prepared to spend a lot of time on their work and to put a lot of effort into it, and they can produce some really impressive pieces.

To help children find out how the paint behaves on silk and how gutta works, it is a good idea to start by letting them do little 'test runs', which can later be used for cards or elasticated hair bands.

Before children begin to paint on silk, they should do a fairly simple drawing without too many details. They should then colour the drawing with ordinary crayons, so that they know in advance which paints the silk version will need.

When the drawing is transferred to the silk, it should be stretched on a small frame with pins.

If the piece of silk gets too large, it can be divided into two or four sections with a line of gutta, in which case all motifs should be drawn onto the silk before it is stretched (see the illustration).

Use a hair-drier to dry the paint quickly (although do not do this with orange or red, which sometimes do not react well to direct heat).

Children can also make elasticated hair bands, buttons, brooches etc. Some examples of paintings produced by children are shown on page 75.

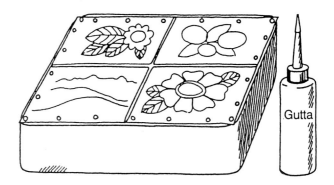

Basic Techniques

On this page and on pages 26 and 27 you will find descriptions of a number of simple techniques, none of which involves the use of gutta. The picture opposite shows the different techniques, which have been used on small scarves. At the foot of this page is a schematic drawing showing the numbers of the scarves, and these numbers refer to the techniques described here. All these methods can be used without stretching the silk on a frame. Instead, the fabric is laid out on wadding, which is placed on a piece of plastic. The advantage with the wadding is that it absorbs the excess paint. The wadding can be washed when there is too much paint on it.

It is important that you read the instructions for these nine techniques carefully, because many of them will be referred to later. Try out the techniques for yourself, and you will learn about the different effects you can achieve.

1. Abstract flowers

- Wet the silk and place it on the wadding.
- Twist little silk points as shown in the illustration below.
- Drop paint onto each point with a pipette so that the paint runs down through the silk and forms flowers. In the picture the first colour used was pink followed by mandarin orange.

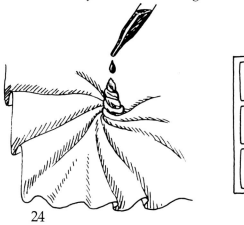

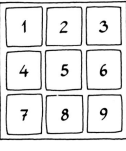

- Drop paint into the gaps using a pipette. The colours used in the picture were emerald green and spring green.

2. Well-defined flowers

- Lay the silk out on the wadding and smooth out all creases.
- Paint the large flowers orange as shown, bearing in mind that the paint will run for at least 1cm (½in). Let the paint dry.
- Paint the medium-sized flowers in mandarin orange and let the paint dry.
- Paint the smallest flowers pink.
- Paint the middle parts of the large and medium-sized flowers pink.
- Paint the middle parts of the small flowers yellow (they will turn red).

3. Checks

- Lay the silk on the wadding and smooth out the creases. If you are going to paint a large section, it is best to stretch the silk on a frame.
- If you want to make sure that the lines are evenly spaced, draw in guidelines first with a fabric marker.
- Dip a fairly large brush – e.g., a no. 12 – in paint. The larger the piece of silk, the bigger brush you will need.
- Start on one side of the scarf and apply the paint in an unbroken movement.
- Brush quickly at first, otherwise the paint may spread too much and there is a danger that you may not have enough paint for the whole line.
- Paint several lines of different colours in succession, making sure that you use the palest colour first and finish with the darkest. Each colour must be dry before you apply the next.

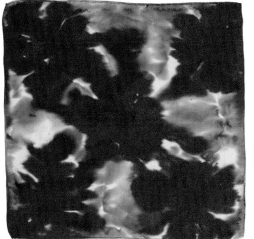 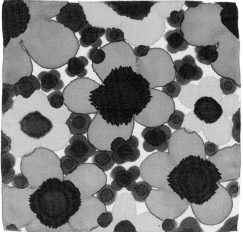 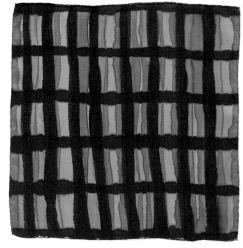

 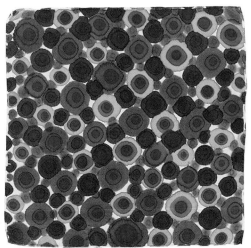 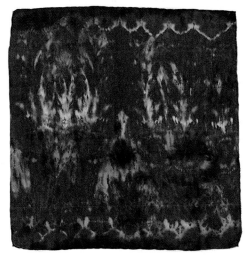

 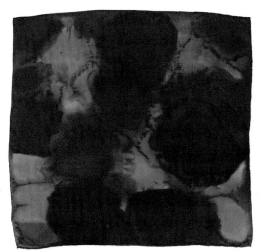 

4. Abstract lines

- Lay the silk on the wadding and smooth out all creases.
- Paint the palest colour onto the silk in broad, wavy lines. Let the paint dry.
- Continue with the next colours – the pale ones first and the dark ones last. Remember to let the paints dry before applying another coat.
- If you want to stop the paint from running, you can use a hair-drier, in which case attach the silk to the wadding with pins and tape to keep it steady. (Remember – never use the hair-drier on orange or red because they may not react well to the heat.)

5. Dots

- Lay the silk out on the wadding and smooth out all the creases.
- Paint large and small dots on the silk. They should not be so large that they run into each other. We began with the pink dots. Allow the paint to dry.
- Paint slightly darker spots – for example, we used azure blue – in the gaps and let the paint dry.
- Continue with smaller dots in a darker colour inside those already painted.
- Carry on until you have achieved the effect you desire.

6. Folding technique in the microwave oven

- Fold the silk concertina-style as shown in the illustration below. Put two or three elastic bands around the silk about every 15cm (6in) to hold in the folds.
- Wash the silk in a bowl containing equal amounts of vinegar and water.
- Squeeze out the water and place the silk in a microwave dish.
- Using three or four paints and, applying them with a pipette, add one colour at a time and make sure the paint goes right into the folds. Start with the palest colours. Darker colours should be used more sparingly.
- Put the lid on the dish.
- Place the dish in the oven for three minutes at 600 watts.
- Take the dish out of the oven and remove the elastic.
- Wash the silk again in the vinegar and water solution
- Roll the silk in a towel to remove moisture and iron it dry.

If you use steam-fixed paints, some manufacturers' paints may be fixed in the microwave oven, in which case it will not be necessary to fix them further. See also the technique on page 36.

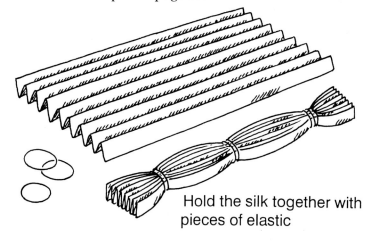

Hold the silk together with pieces of elastic

7. Watercolour

- Lay the silk on the wadding and smooth out all creases.
- Paint the whole surface with watercolour primer, which you can buy in craft shops. The easiest way to apply the primer is with a foam rubber brush. Wait until the primer is dry. Watercolour primers for steam-fixed paints can also be used for iron-fixed paints but always check the manufacturer's instructions.
- Paint flowers and leaves on the silk as shown in the photograph. The silk paint will not run out into the silk but will stay in place exactly as when you are painting watercolours on dry paper.

This method provides a backing for the paint on one side of the silk, which, therefore, has clearly defined right and wrong sides. You cannot use gutta on top of watercolour primer. There are two types of watercolour primer – water-based and spirit-based. The spirit-based watercolour primer is not available in all hobby stores but it is easy to mix yourself from one part transparent spirit-based gutta dissolved in 15 parts of the silk paint thinner supplied by the manufacturer.

There are both advantages and disadvantages with the two types of watercolour primer. The advantage with water-based primer is that it does not smell. Among its disadvantages are that it takes quite a long time to dry, the paint does not stay in place, and it has to be washed out again because the silk becomes stiff.

The advantages of spirit-based watercolour primer are that it dries at lightning speed, the paint stays in place, and it does not need to be washed out. One of the disadvantages is that it has a pungent smell and should therefore always be applied out of doors.

8. Salt-water technique

- Boil a little water with 250g (8oz) salt.
- Strain off any crystals when the salt has dissolved.
- Lay the silk on the wadding and smooth out all creases.
- Paint a base colour over the whole scarf (see page 15). You will get the best effect by using one or more blended colours rather than pure colours.
- Drop salt water on to the scarf with a pipette before the paint is dry. There should be a good distance between the drops. Over the next hour the shapes will begin to change in wonderful ways.
- Wash the silk thoroughly after steam-fixing or iron-fixing. The salt may well make the scarf a little stiff so it is important to wash it out completely.

9. Sugar-water effect

- Boil 0.5 litre (1 pint) of water with 250g (8oz) sugar until it is like syrup. Allow it to cool.
- Lay the silk on the wadding and smooth out all creases.
- Drop syrup on to the scarf with a pipette. There should be a good distance between the drops.
- Drop different colours on to the silk with a pipette.
- If necessary, drop on a little more syrup and then finish off with a dark colour.

When you steam-fix the silk, much of the sugar will disappear as it penetrates the fixing paper.

When you iron-fix your paints wash the silk through with a mild soap in warm water.

Elasticated Hair Bands

These hair bands or scrunchies are quick and easy to make, and they are an excellent way of using left-over scraps of fabric, samples or unsuccessful experiments. For example, you could use the samples described on pages 24–7.

- Cut a piece of silk 40 x 10cm (16 x 4in), although the size will obviously depend on the hair for which it is intended.
- Sew the silk, right sides together, along the long opposite edges to form a tube.
- Turn to the right side.
- Sew the ends together to form a ring, turning in the raw edges, but leave a small opening for a length of elastic to be drawn through.
- Thread the elastic through and tie the ends of the elastic tightly together so that the elastic ring is the right size.
- Close the opening with small overstitches.

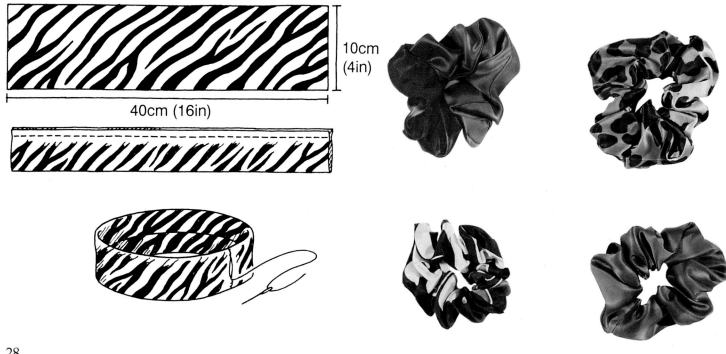

40cm (16in)

10cm (4in)

Scarves

The flowers on this scarf (page 31) were painted without using gutta. However, a line of gutta has been painted around the scarf to create the frame. The instructions for making this frame are given below. It is worth reading this section carefully, because you will need this technique practically every time you make a scarf or a picture.

- Place the scarf on the table with the rolled edge upwards.
- Place a ruler along one rolled edge. Because silk is seldom completely even, there will sometimes be an uneven edge showing above the ruler (see the illustration).
- Hold the ruler firmly in one hand and carefully pull down the silk so that the rolled edge lies right against the ruler.
- Use an autofade fabric marker to draw a line along the opposite side of the ruler as shown in the illustration. The width of the edge depends on the ruler,

and if necessary you can put two rulers together to make it wider or cut a piece of cardboard so that you can make a narrower border.
- Repeat this procedure on the three remaining sides, then stretch the silk on a frame.
- Start in one corner of the frame and make one long line of gutta as far as the next corner.
- Continue with the next side. Make sure that the two lines of gutta overlap slightly at the corners.
- Continue until the whole frame is complete.
- If you wish, use gutta to write your signature in the edge. If you forget to write your signature with gutta or, if you prefer, you can write it with a permanent felt pen after fixing the paint.
- The border is painted **after** the rest of the scarf has been decorated. So that you can paint the scarf edge evenly and without stopping, you will need to remove most of the pins that are holding the silk taut in the frame. Leave a pin in each corner (see illustration).

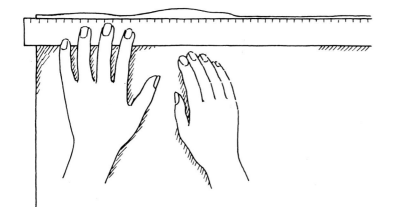
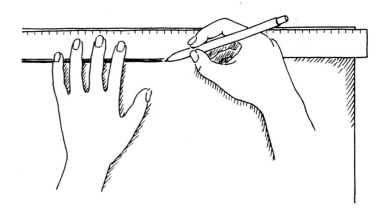

- Put something high underneath the middle of the scarf – e.g., a section of kitchen roll – to raise the centre of the scarf to stop the paint running over the line of gutta.
- Paint the edge in sections as shown in the illustration, using the numbers as a guide to the order of the strokes. It is important that you start in one corner and finish in the opposite one. If you paint one side at a time, the paint will dry unevenly.

Flowers
- Attach the silk to the frame and draw in the gutta line for the border.
- Paint the background inside the frame with a well-thinned grey. If you wish, and to 'lift' the grey, you can paint some large, soft patches of well-thinned red on the still-wet grey background. Leave the paint to dry.
- Paint the flowers in pink – one petal at a time – and let the paint dry.
- Paint the green leaves turquoise and emerald green and let the paint dry.
- Apply some watercolour primer in the centre of each flower and allow to dry (see page 27).
- Use black paint to cover the watercolour primer in the centre of each flower. The primer will set off the flower centres and stop them seeping out into the silk.
- Finally paint the edge black (see left).

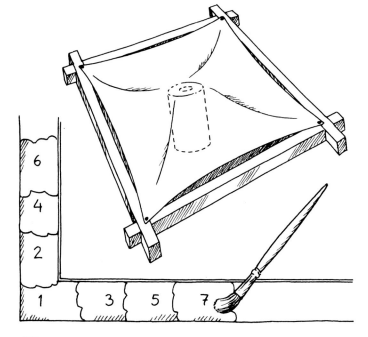

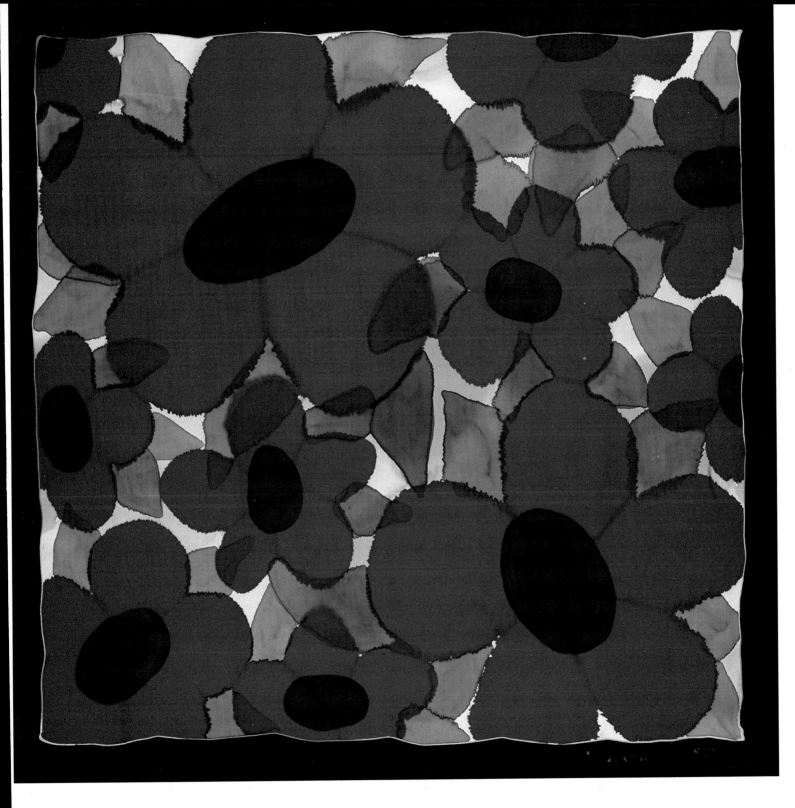

Flowers

Start by drawing the three frames using gutta as explained on pages 29–30.

- Paint the background inside the frame using well-thinned yellow, mandarin orange, orange and pink. Apply the paints wet on wet so that the background will look opalescent.
- Draw the outlines of the flowers with gutta so that they overlap each other and create a three-dimensional effect. Let the colours of the background determine the form of the flowers.
- Draw the outlines of the leaves between the flowers, but do not draw in the veins.
- Fill in the flower petals with yellow, orange, cyclamen and pink. Leave some of the centres of the flowers unpainted so that the background colours can be seen, and paint a dark blue line around the edge of the centres.
- Paint all the leaves spring green.
- Use gutta to draw leaf veins on about half of the leaves as shown in the photograph.
- Paint over the leaves with gutta veins in emerald green.
- Fill in the background between flowers and leaves with black. Make sure that you paint the background last so that you can cover any spots of paint or any paint that has leaked through breaks in the gutta. If the line of gutta is broken in any way, it should be patched up before you apply the black paint.
- Paint the frames, beginning with the inner frame, and ending with the black edge.

Vibeke Born

Fruits

Start by drawing the two frames with gutta as explained on pages 29–30. Pin the silk to a frame.

- Divide the area inside the borders into 16 equal sections as shown in the picture. Use a fabric marker and a long ruler. The ruler should be long enough to rest on the wooden frame when you are drawing the lines.
- Draw the lines with gutta.
- Paint the sections in lightly thinned yellow, mandarin orange, blue and azure blue.
- Draw the fruits with gutta.
- Paint the fruits as shown in the picture. The choice of colours is up to you but some of the colours and techniques are given below.
- Paint the gap between the two outer frames using mandarin orange.
- Draw the apples and cherries with gutta as shown in the picture below.
- Paint the apples pink and the leaves emerald green. The cherries are left in the mandarin orange base colour.

- Paint the background between the apples and the cherries black.
- Paint the edge outside the outer frame using dark blue mixed with a little black.

Colours

Apples: turquoise and blue, applied paint wet on wet.

Slice of melon: emerald green and cyclamen. Paint the flesh in cyclamen red. Outline the seeds with gutta and then fill in with black. Between the emerald green skin and the cyclamen flesh paint a line in a very thin solution of emerald green.

Strawberries: cyclamen and a small amount of blue, applied wet on wet. Draw the spots on the strawberries with gutta while drawing the outline of the fruits i.e., before filling in the berries with colour.

Grapes: colour in the whole bunch with pink or dark blue. When the paint is dry, use gutta to indicate the roundness of the individual grapes, then fill out shapes with pink or dark blue. When the gutta is removed, there will be a slight difference in shade, even if you have used the same colour, because the base colour, used for the bunch, will run into the silk more and will thus become weaker.

Tiger

The colours suggested here are a very simplified description of the colours that can be used. However, you can never know exactly what the background colour will look like on your silk, and it is that very unpredictability that makes silk painting so exciting. You have to experiment for yourself.

Before you begin, twist the silk twice as shown in the illustrations and tie a piece of elastic around the ends to keep the silk twisted.

- Wash the silk in a bowl containing equal amounts of vinegar and water.
- Squeeze out the water and place the silk in a microwave dish with a lid.
- Drop yellow, mandarin orange and lightly thinned orange and sienna paints on the silk using a pipette, working with one colour at a time and making sure that the paint goes right inside the folds. Start with mandarin orange and less of the orange and sienna.
- Cover the dish and put it in the oven for three minutes at 600 watts (steam-fix colours only).
- Take the dish out of the oven and remove the elastic.

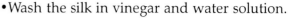

- Wash the silk in vinegar and water solution.
- Roll the silk in a towel and iron it dry as explained on page 19.
- Repeat the whole process if necessary if the scarf colours are not strong enough.
- Draw the two frames with gutta as explained on pages 29–30.
- Working so that the head is in the most lightly coloured corner of the scarf, draw the outline of the whole tiger in gutta.
- Fill in the stripes with black.
- Paint the ears, eyes, teeth, whiskers and under the chin with yellow.
- Paint the nose and tongue cyclamen.
- Paint the chest in a lightly thinned mixture of orange and sienna.
- Thin the mixture you have just used a little more and paint the back of the nose and the back itself.
- Use black to colour the border between the two frames (see illustration).

Vibeke Born

Giraffes

Use sienna and mandarin orange to create the background colour and fix it in the microwave oven as described on page 36.

- Draw the two frames with gutta as explained on pages 29–30.
- Draw in the trees, giraffes and giraffe markings with gutta, using the giraffe pattern on page 50 as a guide.
- Paint the giraffes yellow and mandarin orange and use black for the manes.
- Paint most of the giraffe spots in black, but a few should be brown (refer to the photograph).
- Paint the tree trunks black and the crowns of leaves moss green.

- Paint the sky using a thinned pink mixed with a little dark blue. The colour will look opalescent because the background has already been painted.
- Paint the foreground using a thinned blue.
- Paint the mountains and shadows; we used lilac and dark blue.
- Fill in the border between the two gutta frames with turquoise as shown in the photograph.
- Paint the outer border with black.

38

Mother Giraffe and Young

Paint the whole base with thinned mandarin orange and sienna, applied wet on wet.

- Draw the three frames with gutta as explained on pages 29–30.
- Draw in the large giraffes, spots and the line of the horizon with gutta.
- Paint the giraffe spots black and use brown for the manes.
- Use brown mixed with a little pink for the tongue of the giraffe on the left.
- Paint the top of the ears with a well-thinned grey, and use the same colour for the horns and shadows under the head. Paint the underside of the ears in brown, referring to the photograph as a guide.
- Use well-thinned red to paint around the giraffes and the large giraffe spots.
- Draw in the outlines of the trees, mountains and small giraffes with gutta.
- Paint the tree trunks in brown mixed with a little pink and the tree tops in turquoise.
- Use moss green to paint the grass and a mixture of lilac and dark blue for the mountains.
- Paint the small giraffes black.
- Use orange and pink for the two borders, as shown in the picture.
- Paint the outside edge in black.

40

Vibeke Born

Zebras in a Rainbow

Start by drawing the inner frame with gutta as explained on pages 29–30.

- Use gutta to draw the zebras, the curved horizon and the two vertical lines (refer to the illustration below as a guide).
- Paint the two outer zebras black.
- Paint the middle zebra grey.
- Draw horizontal lines in gutta on the middle zebra.
- Paint the black stripes as shown in the photograph.
- Paint the ground under the horizon using thinned emerald green.
- Paint hillocks using various unthinned shades of green.
- Paint the left-hand section yellow, the central section red and the right-hand section blue (we used azure blue).
- Draw vertical lines of gutta in the three sections over the zebras. (These are shown as dotted lines in the illustration below.)

- Paint the left-hand section in various shades of yellow and orange.
- Paint the central section in various shades of pink and red.
- Paint the right-hand section in various shades of blue and green.
- Use mandarin orange, cyclamen and dark blue respectively to fill in the areas beneath the three zebras.
- Paint the border using blue and turquoise.

42

Zebra Fantasy

Begin by drawing the outer frame with gutta as explained on pages 29–30.

- Draw the zebras, the inner frame and the rest of the design with gutta. Use the zebra stripes on page 51 as an additional guide.
- Apply a grey background, then paint the horizontal black stripes at the bottom.
- Paint the zebras and the individual sections in blue and the manes, heads, noses and back legs in dark blue.
- Use a fabric marker to put some crosses in the sections to be painted black and then paint them. If you are unlucky and the black seeps through a broken line of gutta, you will have to make an extra stripe and fill it in with black.
- Mark the sections you want to be grey, then paint them.
- Draw the stripes on the grey base with gutta and paint them black.
- Fill in the border between the two outer frames with blue.
- Draw a gutta frame on top of the blue and paint the innermost section dark blue.
- Finally paint the edge black.

44

Vibeke Born

Leopards

Begin by drawing the three frames with gutta as explained on pages 29–30

- Divide the area inside the innermost frame into four equal horizontal sections. The horizontal lines between the sections should be drawn as double lines.
- Use gutta to draw the outlines of the leopards, and also to draw the lowest horizontal line, behind the leopards in the bottom section.
- Paint the ground under the gutta line just painted with a mixture of brown and orange.
- Paint the leopards, the third section and the inner band of the border with a well-thinned mixture of sienna and mandarin orange. Paint shadows wet on wet on the leopards and border with a very thin solution of grey.
- Paint the central band of the frame orange as shown in the photograph.
- Paint the top horizontal section with lightly thinned sienna.
- Paint around the leopards in the second and bottom sections with a well thinned sienna.
- Paint the thin, horizontal stripes in the gaps black.

- Draw the trees, horizon and paths in the bottom section with gutta.
- Paint the trees, middle ground and paths orange, black and brown mixed with a little black.
- Use a foam rubber brush to paint the whole scarf as far as the middle section with watercolour primer (see page 27). Let the primer dry.
- Paint spots in the first and third sections with sienna.
- Paint around the spots using brown mixed with black as shown in the picture.
- Paint black spots on the leopards and in the inner frame section.
- Finally paint the edge outside the outer frame using brown mixed with black.

Cushions

The cushions described on this and the next two pages are painted on satin like the ties on pages 68–9. So, if you paint extra material, you will also have enough for a tie and, for example, an elastic hair band and card (see page 28 and pages 70–71). If you want to paint larger pieces of silk to make up into clothes, you can stretch the silk on two trestles as explained on page 12.

This section explains how to make a leopard, a giraffe and a zebra cushion. If you want to make a tiger cushion as shown in the photograph, paint the base wet on wet using yellow and mandarin orange. Draw the stripes with gutta and fill them in with black.

Leopard Cushion

- Paint the whole base with a thin solution of sienna and mandarin orange. Thin the paint as necessary throughout so that the base colour will shimmer.
- Paint watercolour primer (see page 27) on the whole piece and let the primer dry.
- Paint spots with a mixture of brown and black (see also the leopard spots on page 47).

48

Giraffe Cushion

- Paint the whole base with a mixture of yellow, mandarin orange and a little orange thinned with a small amount of water. Thin the paint as necessary throughout so that the base colour will shimmer.
- Draw the outline of the spots with gutta.
  Fill in the spots with black.

Zebra Cushion

- Draw the pattern with gutta.
- Use a fabric marker to indicate the sections for the various colours.
- Paint the different sections with mandarin orange, lightly thinned sienna, pure sienna, grey, black and brown mixed with orange.

Toucans on a Pink Background

Begin by drawing the two frames with gutta as explained on pages 29–30.

- Draw the outline of the toucans with gutta, including the outline of the breast patch.
- Paint the beak and the top of the head with mandarin orange.
- Paint the shaded part of the breast a thinned grey.
- Draw the line across the beak, the outline of the spot on the beak, and also the eye and pupil with gutta.
- Paint the bottom part of the beak orange.
- Paint the inner eye, the spot on the beak and the body black.
- Paint the background around the birds and the inner border with thinned red mixed with a little black.
- Draw in the outlines of the feet of the birds and also branches and leaves with gutta.
- Paint the branches and the feet black.
- Mix pink with black for the leaves.
- Draw a gutta frame on top of the pink base in the border between the outer frames and paint the outer section with the same mixture of colours as the leaves.
- Finally paint the edge black.

52

Vibeke Born

Yellow and Blue Parrots

Begin by drawing the two frames with gutta as explained on pages 29–30. The frames are broken in two places, as you can see in the photograph.

- Draw the parrots and branches with gutta.
- Paint the parrots using yellow, emerald green, azure blue, blue, dark blue and black. Paint the tops of the heads wet on wet with blue and yellow. Paint the shaded breast sections wet on wet with a very thin solution of grey. Paint the feet with a very thin mixture of grey and brown.
- Use gutta to draw in the outlines of the feathers on one of the birds.
- Then paint over the azure blue with dark blue.
- Paint the branches with a mixture of dark blue and a little black.
- Paint the background of the parrots and the branches with lilac.
- Paint the central section the frame in yellow.
- Draw a gutta frame on the yellow base and paint the inner section of the frame emerald green.
- Finally paint the outside edge dark blue.

54

Viveka Bronn

Parakeets

Begin by drawing the two frames with gutta as explained on pages 29–30.

- Draw the birds, branches and leaves with gutta.
- Paint the head of each bird red. Paint the beak pink and paint above the beak with thinned mandarin orange. Use this colour for the feet as well.
- Paint the inner section of the frame pink.
- Paint the birds' bodies wet on wet with a mixture of spring green and yellow and also with pure yellow.
- Paint the eyes and the branches black.
- Paint the leaves dark blue. To vary the colours a little, paint some of the leaves twice to make the colour darker.
- Draw a gutta frame on the pink base and paint the inner border black.
- Finally paint the edge black.

Vibeke Born

Penguins

Begin by drawing the frame with gutta as explained on pages 29–30.
- Draw the penguins, mountains and ice floes with gutta.
- Paint the heads, wings, backs and feet of the large penguins black.
- Apply lightly thinned mandarin orange to the heads.
- Paint the shaded breast sections with a very thin solution of mandarin orange.
- Paint the bottom part of the bodies grey.
- Paint the penguins in the background black with grey feet.
- Paint the baby penguin in grey and black.
- Paint the dark water with a mixture of dark blue and blue.
- Thin this mixture and use it for the light blue sections.
- Paint the grey sections.
- Finish by painting the outer border black.

58

Vibeke Born. 90.

Lemurs

Begin by drawing the curved outer frame with gutta as explained on pages 29–30.

- Draw the outlines of the lemurs, their eyes and the curvy inner frame with gutta. Also use gutta to draw the stripes on the frame and on the tails.
- Paint the bodies of the lemurs with a lightly thinned grey.
- Paint the shaded sections on the lemurs with a very thin solution of sienna.
- Paint all the eyes with mandarin orange.
- Draw the pupils with gutta.
- Paint the noses, the insides of the ears, the tops of the heads and also the pupils and stripes black.
- Paint the whole of the background around the lemurs and the eyes spring green.
- Draw in the leaves with gutta, then paint them emerald green.
- Finally paint the edge black.

60

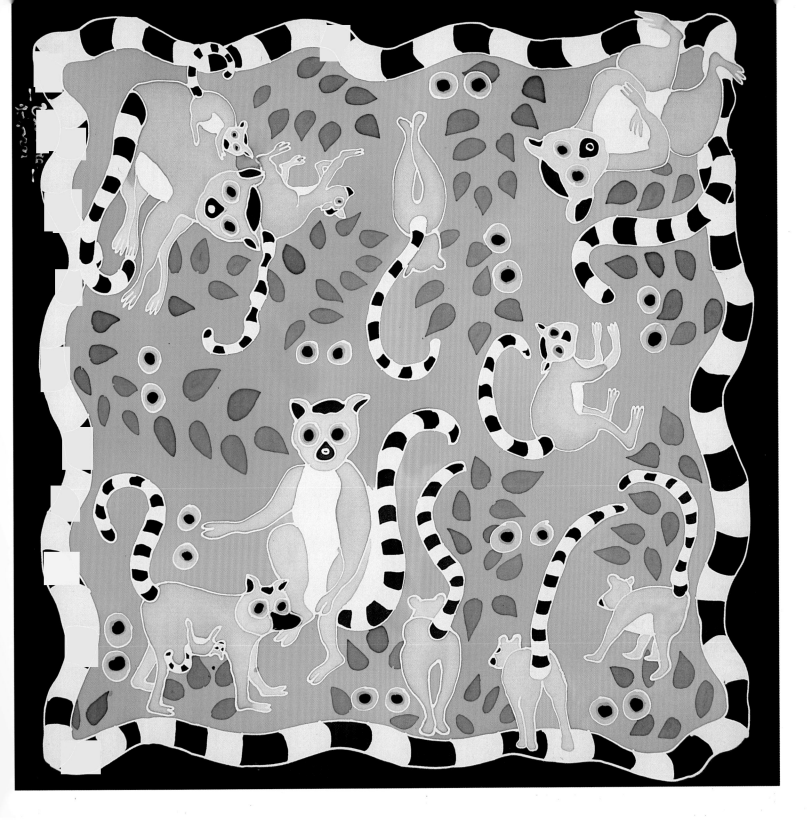

Clown Fish

Begin by drawing the two frames with gutta as explained on pages 29–30.

- Draw the outline of the fish with gutta. Then use gutta to draw the eyes and the lines marking off the heads, gills, middle sections and tails.
- Paint the sections between the gutta lines using orange and mandarin orange.
- Paint the gap between frames orange.
- Draw gutta lines roughly 5mm (¼in) from the outer edges of the orange sections.
- Fill in the areas with black.
- Paint the background around the fish wet on wet with azure blue, blue and dark blue.
- Draw a gutta frame on the orange inner frame and paint the inside section of the frame black.
- Finally paint the outside edge black.

62

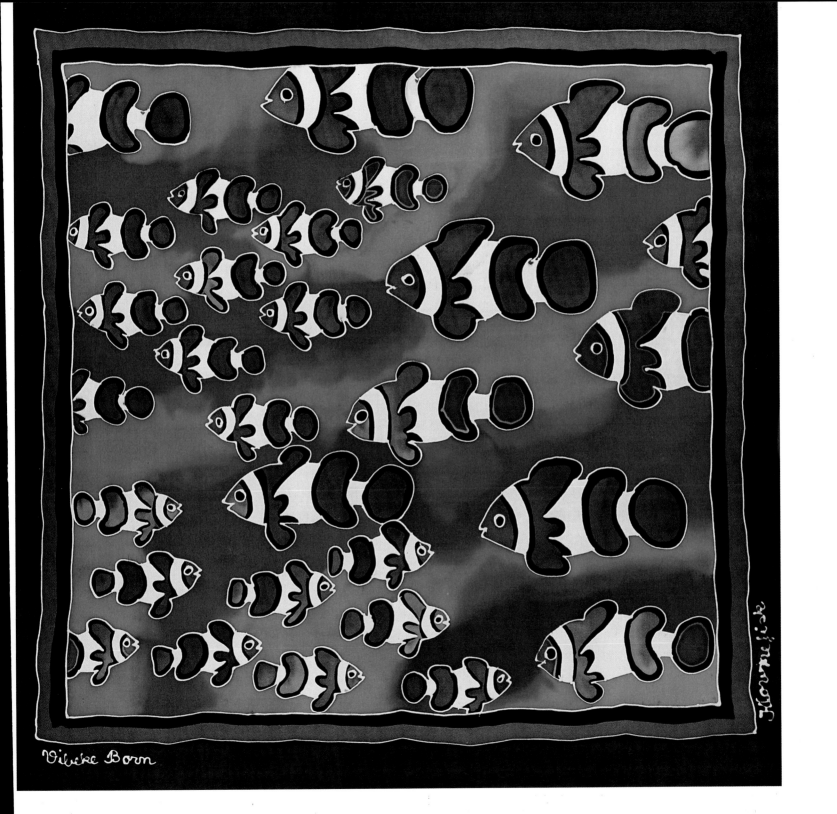

Vibeke Born

Toucans on a Blue Background

Begin by drawing the two frames with gutta as explained on pages 29–30.

- Draw the toucans and the branches with gutta.
- Paint the toucans, the branches and the background as shown in the photograph. There are many possible combinations of form and colour, and you should choose whichever colours you like, especially for the beaks. Look carefully at the photograph and compare it with the techniques we have used in earlier projects; you will not find it difficult to achieve an attractive and exciting result.
- Draw the inner border as shown in the illustration.

Pandas

The pandas illustrated below are the same as the ones shown on the front cover of this book. Begin by drawing the two frames with gutta as explained on pages 29–30.

- Draw the pandas with gutta and fill in the bodies with black and a very thin solution of grey for the shaded sections.
- Paint the background as shown in the photograph, draw in the gutta lines and fill in the details of trees and flowers.

Vibeke Born

Ties

In some craft shops you can buy silk ties that are ready made up for you to paint on. Lighter weight ties may go out of shape if too much paint is applied. If you do decide that you want to experiment with a ready-made tie, try and buy the best quality you can. When painting onto ready-made ties you will probably find it easier to use iron-fixed paints as steaming the tie may cause it to shrink and twist.

The photograph opposite shows some of the ways in which ties can be decorated with paints.

The ties in the picture have been painted on satin before being sewn. You can also use crepe de Chine, but lightweight habutai silk is too thin.

Instructions on making up a tie are included below. It can be a little tricky if you have not had much experience with a sewing machine.

- Draw a pattern for the tie as shown in the diagram, which is to a scale of 1 : 5. Also draw a pattern for the interfacing, which is shown by the shaded area.
- Cut out the tie from a length of silk and also cut a lining.
- Cut a piece of iron-on interfacing.
- Iron the interfacing in place on the lining.

- With the tie and lining right sides together, stitch the two pieces together, leaving the wide end at the bottom open. Trim the lining so that it is about 2.5cm (1in) shorter than the silk.
- Turn the tie to the right side and press.
- Turn up the wide end by about 2.5cm (1in), and the narrow end by about 12mm (½in).
- Turn under a narrow hem in the silk, making sure that the V-shapes are symmetrical. Press the silk to the lining and slip stitch in place, making sure that the stitches do not come through to the right side.

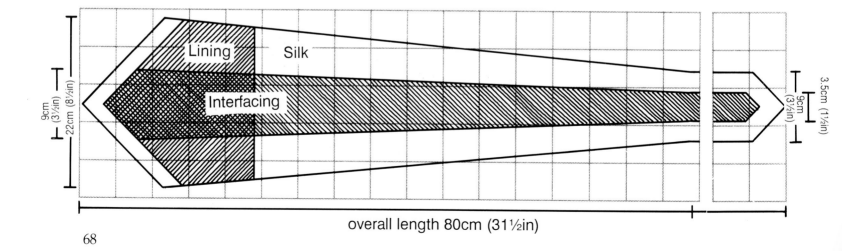

9cm (3½in)
22cm (8½in)

Lining   Silk

Interfacing

3.5cm (1½in)
9cm (3½in)

overall length 80cm (31½in)

Cards and Small Pictures

Rather than paint just one card at a time, it is much easier to stretch a large piece of silk, 90 x 90cm (36 x 36in), on a frame.

Divide the silk into suitable sections – either as shown in the photograph or as shown in the illustration below. The silk shown in the photograph has been divided into horizontal sections with gutta. After painting the silk, cut it into horizontal strips along the gutta lines, and then cut smaller, vertical pieces from the strip to create cards as shown in the photograph on page 73 (second row).

The illustration below shows you how you can also divide up the whole piece of silk with gutta into smaller

sections both horizontally and vertically to create patterned pieces that can be used for cards and pictures.

For cards you should use a good quality satin, crepe de Chine or habutai. The paint colours look their best on a strong silk. You do not need to fix the paints because the cards and pictures will not come in contact with water. However, you should bear in mind that steam-fixing does make the silk more brilliant and the colour deeper.

When you paint on silk and cut it out for mounting as a card, you must make sure that there is a suitable border that can be covered with tape or the front of the card. Use spray or stick adhesive sparingly. Alternatively, hold the edges of the fabric down with adhesive tape.

The best kinds of adhesive to use are the low-tack kinds that allow you to move the fabric about until you are absolutely satisfied with the position of the silk under the frame. If you use a spray adhesive, make sure that you work in a well-ventilated room or, ideally, outdoors because the fumes are unpleasant and they can be dangerous.

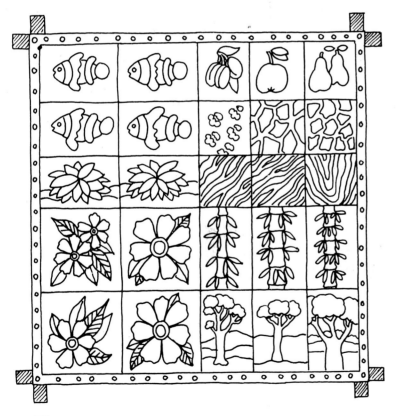

Framed Cards

Making cards is the ideal way of using up scraps of fabric – perhaps some experiments that didn't quite work or pieces that you have cut off larger pieces of material. Although you can buy ready-made blanks, it is easy to make your own, and this gives you the opportunity to choose coloured card that complements your silk and to cut out shapes that are appropriate for the design.

The illustration shows a variety of cards with square, triangular, diamond-shaped, round and other cut-outs. Use a craft knife, and remember to draw the lines on the reverse of the card, measuring them carefully. Divide the card into three equal sections, and remember that the aperture needs to be cut in the right-hand section so that, when it is bent over the central section, it becomes the front, with the left-hand section bent the other way to form the back of the card.

Use low-tack spray adhesive or adhesive stick to hold the silk in place on the central section, and if you wish, place a small amount of padding behind the silk.

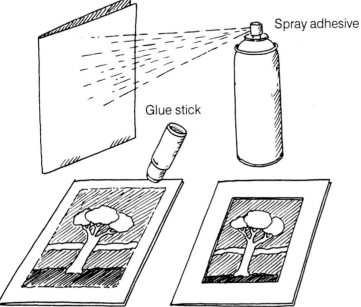

Spray adhesive

Glue stick

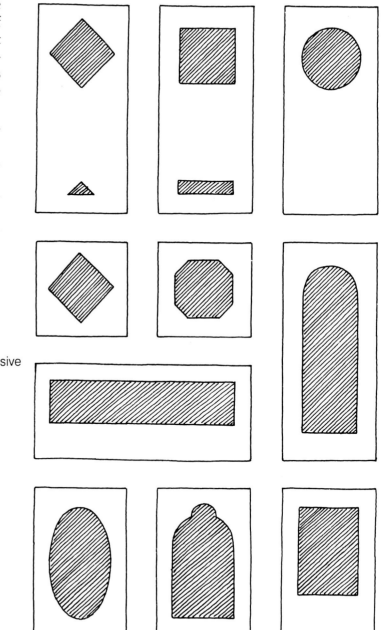

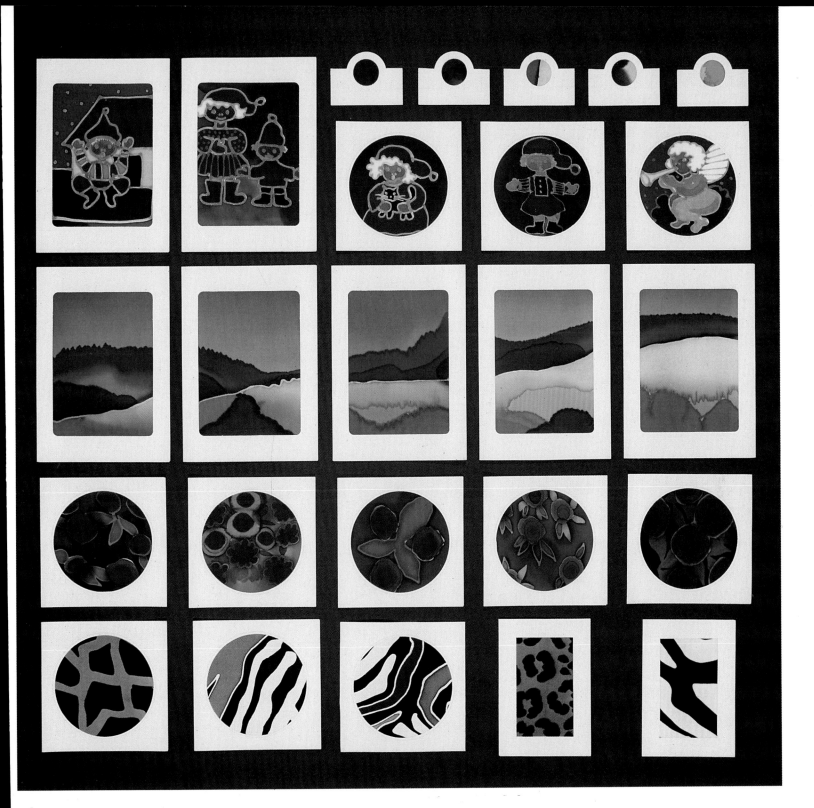

Children's Paintings

The paintings in the photograph on page 75 are the work of children between the ages of five and twelve. Children love using silk paints because of the wonderful way they blend together and the beautiful colours that can be created.

The drawings, which should transferred to the silk with a fabric marker, should be very simple. Unless the silk is a fairly large piece, when it can be divided with gutta into four or more sections, the silk can be stretched in an embroidery frame or even over a small wooden box.

Before children begin to work on a special motif or picture, let them experiment with scraps of similar quality silk and the same kind of paints so that they can get a feel for the ways in which the materials work together and begin to understand the kinds of effects that can be achieved.

Pour the paints into a palette. If you put paint in alternate dishes, the empty dishes can be used for mixing colours.

Remember, always supervise children carefully because some paints and gutta are slightly toxic. Follow the manufacturer's instructions.

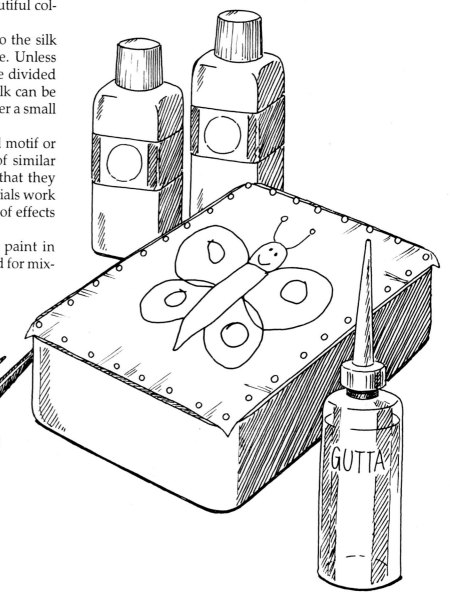

SUPPLIERS

PAINT & MATERIALS

The following suppliers also offer a mail order service:

UNITED KINGDOM

George Weil & Sons Ltd (shop)
18 Hanson Street
London W1P 7DB
Tel 0171 580 3763

(MAIL ORDER - WORLDWIDE)
The Warehouse
Reading Arch Road
Redhill
Surrey RH1 1HG
England
Tel 01737 778868

Green and Stone
259 Kings Road
London SW3 5EL
Tel 0171 352 0837

(MAIL ORDER ONLY)
Panduro Hobby Ltd
Westway House
Transport Avenue
Brentford
Middlesex
Tel 0181 847 6161

UNITED STATES & CANADA

Rupert Gibbon & Spider
PO Box 425
Healdsburg
CA 95448
Tel 707 433 9577
Fax 707 433 4906

SOUTH AFRICA

Silk Art
8 Uitsig Close
Fairtrees
Durbanville 7550
Tel 021 960205
Fax 021 9751196

AUSTRALIA & NEW ZEALAND

Silk Screen Fabrics Ltd
127 Pilkington Road
Panmure
Auckland 6
New Zealand
Tel 09 570 4366
Fax 09 570 5399

Marie France H O
92 Currie Street
Adelaide
SA 5000
Tel 08 231 4138

Silk Road
PO Box 180
Bega
NSW 2550
Tel 064 924 587

STEAM FIXING

SUPPLIERS OF PAINTS CAN USUALLY ADVISE ABOUT PLACES WHERE YOU CAN GET YOUR WORK FIXED PROFESSIONALLY.

The following offer professional steam-fixing services:

UNITED KINGDOM

Isabel Hanmer
c/o The Frame Factory
20 Cross Street
London NW1 2BJ

UNITED STATES

Shirley Waxman
7531 Coddle Harbor Ln
Potomac
MD 20854
Tel 301 299 5526

Design Originals by Beverly Hicks
12872 Olive Street
Garden Grove
CA 92645
Tel 714 892 2323

SOUTH AFRICA

Silk Art
8 Uitsig Close
Fairtrees
Durbanville 7550
Tel 021 960205
Fax 021 9751196

AUSTRALIA & NEW ZEALAND

Marie France
223 High Streeet
Kew
VIC 3101
Tel 039 853 2668

Lynne Britten
17 Edward Street
Charlestown
NSW 2290
049 431860

Published in Australia and New Zealand in 1995 by Kangaroo Press Pty Ltd
3 Whitehall Road, Kenthurst, NSW 2156, Australia
PO Box 6125, Dural Delivery Centre, NSW 2158

ISBN 0 86417 731 3

Danish edition © 1993 Forlaget Klematis: Silkemaling idé og inspiration

English edition © 1995 David Porteous

Translated by Tim Bowler.
Printed and bound in Singapore.